TABLE
OF THE
LORD

To Ted,

With hearty gratitude
for your partnership
in the Body and
ministry of Christ.

Jack
3/17/84

TABLE OF THE LORD

Holy
Communion
in the Life
of the
Church

Alvin N. Rogness

AUGSBURG Publishing House • Minneapolis

Contents

Preface

Most people of my age grew up at a time when Holy Communion was celebrated three or four times a year. In my 20 years as a parish pastor, we never had Communion at a regular morning service, even in the festival seasons, always at a separate time for people who made it a point to come. Never did we usher a whole Sunday morning congregation to the altar. Today most congregations have the Lord's Supper at their regular services, usually once a month, even more often in some churches.

Where communicants come as they do today, without private confession and perhaps little preparation, often unaware that there is Communion until they enter the church, does the Supper become so casual that its solemn character is all but lost? Moreover, will renewed accent on the sacrament lead to a diminished concern for the preaching of the Word?

These are questions that leave me uneasy. I would deplore the loss of the sacrament's solemnity. I would deplore even more the loss of preaching of the Word as the heart of a congregation's worship.

Whether the Spirit is moving the church toward a richer ministry, I leave to the judgment of time and experience. Meanwhile it is of importance that through devout discipline we retain, or perhaps recover, the riches of grace that the sacrament gives. It is to this end that this little book is offered.

1

The Solemn Moment

There are many ways to worship. For the Christian, Holy Communion holds a unique place. It is the only form which Jesus specifically asked of his followers, "Take and eat . . . drink . . . in remembrance of me." Whether on that Thursday night at the Passover meal he envisaged the central place Holy Communion would have in his church 2000 years later, we cannot know. But today in virtually every branch of his church, Communion is the most solemn moment of its worship. For many it may not be the most stirring act of worship. Great preaching and inspiring hymns may move people more deeply. But for the church as a whole Communion has become the point where Christ's death for the sins of the world is brought into the most ineffable and concrete focus: "this is my body broken for you; this is my blood shed for you."

It was a bewildered and anxiety-filled band of disciples that sat around the table with Jesus that night. Even before coming to Jerusalem for the Passover, they had a hunch that tragedy awaited their master. They had cautioned, even protested, his going. But Jesus told them that his time had come; he had to go. Quite openly he told them that his death was imminent, and that his death was a necessary piece in God's larger plan.

From the moment of his arrival in Jerusalem, events moved swiftly. For three years rumors of this man from Nazareth had spread through the country. His bold teaching and his miraculous works had given rise in many to the hope that at long last a leader, the Messiah, had come who would deliver the nation from the oppression of Rome and restore the glory of Israel.

When Jesus rode into the city that Sunday, great excitement surged through the crowd. They threw their garments and palm branches in his path and hailed him as the successor to their great king David. The abortive moment of triumph was short-lived. His enemies, leaders in Israel who feared that any ill-conceived resistance to Rome would, as before, only harden the oppressor's hand, had already plotted to have Jesus die. They had found an unexpected agent in one of Jesus' own disciples, Judas, who had agreed to deliver him into their hands. Thursday night was the time.

After carefully arranging a secret meeting place, Jesus had succeeded in having this last supper with his twelve, the men who for the better part of three years had been his constant companions. Peter was there, and John and James, Andrew and Philip, Bartholomew, Matthew, Thomas, James the son of Alphaeus, Thaddaeus, Simon, and Judas Iscariot.

The meal over, Jesus left his place at the table, took a basin of water and a towel and proceeded to do what traditionally the lowest servant of a household would do. He washed and dried the disciples' feet, one after another, to the embarrassment of his men. Returning to the table, he spoke to them of his own role as a servant and reminded them that if no service was too lowly for him, neither should any loving service be too lowly for them.

Then he took the bread and the cup.

Could they, or the church after them, ever forget the mysterious words and the touch of bread and wine on their lips, "This is my body . . . this is my blood of the covenant"?

Later that night came Gethsemane, the arrest, in the early morning his trial before Pilate, and then Calvary, where his body was broken and his blood was shed.

We come to the Lord's Table in simple obedience: "take and eat . . . drink . . . do this in remembrance of me." We cannot possibly plumb the depths of the mystery of the sacrament, to say nothing of the mystery of God's strange and endless love for us. But we come, because he has invited and commanded us to come. For anyone who desires seriously to be a follower of Jesus, this is enough.

Obviously there is more. Our Lord would not have us do something with no meaning, no benefits, no blessing. There is more to the sacrament than a mere test of obedience. The Holy Spirit has led the church to have this single act filled with such rich grace that it has fed the souls of hundreds of millions with indefinable comfort and strength. If it had been only a commemorative act, like raising the country's flag on holidays, it would long since have disappeared from the life of the church. It is a *sacrament,* instituted by Christ himself, through which by visible means he conveys and affirms his invisible grace. The sacrament conveys the living Redeemer, not merely some new truth.

It is not a memorial for someone dead and gone; it is an occasion with someone still alive, someone who is our very life, someone still present with us and acting in us.

It is an act, not a lesson, the act of Christ present in his church. It is not the hour of instruction; it is the hour of communion.

For I received from the Lord what I also delivered to you, that the Lord Jesus on the night when he was betrayed took bread, and when he had given thanks, he broke it, and said, "This is my body which is for you. Do this in remembrance of me." In the same way also the cup, after supper, saying, "This cup is the new covenant in my blood. Do this, as often as you drink it, in remembrance of me." For as often as you eat this bread and drink the cup, you proclaim the Lord's death until he comes.

1 Cor. 11:23-26

> Lord Jesus Christ, you have prepared
> This feast for my salvation,
> Your very body and your blood;
> Thus, at your invitation,
> With weary heart, by sin oppressed,
> I come to you for needed rest;
> I need your peace, your pardon.
> *LBW 208*

You were not really saying good-bye to your disciples that night, were you, O Lord? You knew that you would rise to see them again, and to be with us all forever. With your enemies at the door and with death only hours away, your heart bled for Peter and John and the others. And your heart bleeds for us, whose spirits are heavy with fear. You have given us this Supper of bread and wine to remember many things—above all, that you are here in your body and blood. Thank you for inviting us to eat and drink. Amen.

2

The Setting

Lord Arthur Balfour, British philosopher-statesman, once said, "A religion that is small enough for our understanding would not be large enough for our needs." Everything we believe and do in the Christian faith lies beyond the limits of neat demonstrable understanding.

We trust a God whom we've never seen or touched or heard, and we talk to him. The book, the Bible, which by normal standards is much like other kinds of literature, we regard as the Word of God, the God whom we cannot see. We worship as Lord a young carpenter from Nazareth, whom we believe to be both fully God and fully human. And in Holy Communion we taste bread and wine, but believe that we receive his body and blood. We are, in Peter's words, a peculiar people.

When those who have never worshiped with Christians enter the church at the service of Communion, they may understandably be puzzled. Why are these people standing or kneeling before the altar to eat a bit of bread and sip the wine? They might conceivably understand the ethical exhortations of the sermon and perhaps enjoy the cadences of the great hymns. But this strange act? What can that mean? Not until they grasp the setting—the staggering story behind the Supper—would they have an inkling of the solemn event of the sacrament.

And what a dramatic setting it has. The whole sweep of the faith somehow comes to focus. These people, these peculiar people, believe that the vast universe of billions of bodies in billions of light years of space has a maker whom they call God. They believe that this God colonized an island called earth with his sons and daughters and gave to them the unique gift of choice, the right to obey or disobey, a gift he gave to nothing else in the universe (except to angels), neither to the galaxies that roll, the birds that fly, or the fish that swim. They also believe that the troubles on earth stem from people's disobedience, which separates them from their God in a separation so profound that by themselves they cannot possibly return to him.

It is at this point in the drama that the action moves toward its climax. God did not give up on them. These were his children, he loved them, and he wanted them back with him. To achieve this, he entered the world of human beings; he invaded the earth, in the person of his only Son, who took his place among the human family. He became human, born of woman. He assumed the sin and guilt of the separated children and gave his body and blood in death on a cross in some strange and wonderful way to forgive their sins, snatch them out of bondage to sin, death, and the power of the devil, in order that they could live under him in a kingdom of God intended for them from the beginning.

Moreover, they believe that this son of Mary and Son of God arose from the dead, ascended to heaven and lives and reigns forever. They also believe—these peculiar people—that this Lord, Jesus of Nazareth, established a new colony on earth, his church, and in the church instituted the sacraments of Baptism and Holy Communion, and that these with the Word of God (in the Scriptures and in preaching) are the means or channels which the Spirit uses to summon the children back to God and keep them in fellowship with him.

What fantasy is this? one might ask. It is the faith of Christians. It is, in part at least, the setting for what they do when they come to Holy Communion.

Mystery? Yes, indeed. What person's feeble understanding could possibly have arrived at this exalted assessment of human beings? Our home is a tiny speck in the vast universe. There are four billion of us swarming on this little ball, often despoiling the earth and destroying one another. We appear for all the world like any other species of animal life, in a grim and irrational struggle for survival. How can

God have a special stake in these mammals? How can they be children of the almighty God who loves them and destines them for an eternity with him?

Let no one say, "I will not believe until I can understand." We will never understand; we must believe without understanding, if we are to believe at all. Until the end, and however flaming our faith, we will stand in wonder and awe before the mystery of the universe, its God and God's love for humankind.

Robert Millikan, winner of the Nobel Prize in physics, once said, "When I view the universe, its microcosm and macrocosm, its incredible order, and ponder its vast unknown and unknowable, I join the psalmist of old and say, 'The heavens declare the glory of God and the firmament showeth forth his handiwork.'" Every sensitive, intelligent person can join Millikan. But it takes a radical miracle of faith to believe that this God—hidden and yet revealed in the amazing order, power, and beauty of nature's universe—created us human beings to be uniquely his children eternally, and that he became human and went to the lengths of a cross to recover us.

Once having brought into view the incredible setting of what we believe about God and humanity, the Lord's Supper itself will fit very neatly into the whole. To receive the bread and say, "Now I have received his body broken for me," and the wine, "Now I have received his blood shed for me," will only add to the wonder and mystery of God's measureless love for his children.

He is the image of the invisible God, the first-born of all creation; for in him all things were created, in heaven and on earth, visible and invisible, whether thrones or dominions or principalities or authorities— all things were created through him and for him. He is before all things, and in him all things hold together. He is the head of the body, the church; he is the beginning, the first-born from the dead, that in everything he might be pre-eminent. For in him all the fulness of God was pleased to dwell, and through him to reconcile to himself all things, whether on earth or in heaven, making peace by the blood of his cross.

Col. 1:15-20

Of the glorious body telling,
O my tongue, its mysteries sing,
And the blood, all price excelling,
Which the world's eternal King
In a noble womb once dwelling,
Shed for this world's ransoming.
    LBW 120

It sends my little mind spinning, O God, to think that in this vast universe you have your eye on me. And to think that your love has reached down to me in your only Son, and that he has died for me! I will not try to fathom the mystery. Help me to snuggle into it, as a bird under the wing of its mother. Help me to stay there, whatever happens to me. Amen.

3

Symbol

For a part of the Christian family the bread and wine are viewed as symbols, reminders of the Lord's death on Calvary. The Supper helps them to remember him as he lived and died and rose again centuries ago. He was once present on earth in bodily form; he will come again in glory—(in bodily form)— in the meantime he is seated in majesty at the right hand of the Father. Between these two bodily appearances, he is now "spiritually" present in the lives of believers.

The concept of the sacrament as "mere symbol" and Christ's presence among us only as a presence in the hearts of believers has not been enough for most of the Christian church. The question of *how* Christ is present in the sacrament has generated controversy among theologians of the churches—a subject we will come to later.

It may not be fair or accurate to say *mere* symbol. Symbols are something we can touch or taste or hear or see, but they carry us beyond themselves. A photograph of a friend, for instance, is more than a piece of cardboard covered with sensitive paper on which an image has been made. When I look at a photograph of our daughter when she was six, the picture conjures up in my memory a whole world of tenderness and love. The print is not our daughter. It is a symbol, but obviously much more. The flag of my country is but cloth with colored stars and stripes; it is not the country itself. But as it is raised to the call of a bugle, my spirit is deeply moved to gratitude and pride by reflection on what it means to be a citizen.

Ian Maclaren tells of a great and good man who was honored for his service to his city. They raised a statue of him and erected it in the open street. His virtues were written underneath so that all the city should remember. When the statue was unveiled, the eyes of many people were wet with tears, but the eyes of the members of his family were dry. For that official-looking figure in the unfamiliar, flowering robes cut in marble was not that of the father they loved. At home they had dearer, far more intimate symbols, which brought him back vividly to their minds and hearts. A Bible, a portrait, a pack of letters—these meant much more.

In some sense, it is so with Jesus. His statue, as it

were, has been raised from earth to heaven. His influence is woven into the fabric of the world's life. But for those who love him, as for the disciples, the intimate symbols of bread and wine are the ones that stir most deeply.

Long ago a homeless lad was brought into a children's home. They gave him a new suit, new stockings, new shoes. But when they offered him a new cap, he drew back, clinging to the old ragged one in his hand. When they wouldn't allow him to keep it, he tore the lining out and stuffed it in his pocket. "Why did you do that," they asked. With tears in his eyes, he said, "Because the lining of my old cap was part of my mother's dress. It's all I have left of her, and somehow it seems to bring her back." Perhaps that's something of what *sacramental* means.

For me Christ's presence as symbol alone does not say enough. Nor am I satisfied only with his spiritual presence in my heart. The instruction I have had about the sacrament, ever since confirmation class, has led me to expect more. On the other hand, I am sure that my friends whose instruction has emphasized his symbolic presence alone and for whom the Supper is chiefly to remember Calvary, may come at the Lord's invitation with as deep a sense of obedience and reverence as I. Even I, who believe that the Lord is indeed present in the bread and wine with his body and blood, find that the act of remembering all he did for me long ago through his death and resurrection is a moving part of my worship.

What he *did* for us is, after all, most important.

I am not saved by eating and drinking his body and blood; I am saved because he came to Bethlehem, died at Calvary, and rose again that first Easter morning. His finished work is my hope. It is not the bread and wine which the pastor consecrates, it is not the sacred aura of the meal, it is not my repentance or my feelings of his presence that is my salvation. The Communion is a gift, a wonderful gift of blessing. But I am his because he died for me long ago. To remember this—if it's the only thing I do—is a very high act of worship.

Remember Jesus Christ, risen from the dead, descended from David, as preached in my gospel, the gospel for which I am suffering and wearing fetters like a criminal. But the word of God is not fettered. Therefore I endure everything for the sake of the elect, that they also may obtain the salvation which in Christ Jesus goes with eternal glory. The saying is sure: If we have died with him, we shall also live with him; if we endure, we shall also reign wth him; if we deny him, he will also deny us; if we are faithless, he remains faithful—for he cannot deny himself.

2 Timothy 2:8-13

Jesus, I will ponder now
On your holy Passion;
Let your Spirit now endow
Me for meditation.
Grant that I in love and faith

May the image cherish
Of your suffering, pain, and death,
That I may not perish.
LBW 115

Lord Jesus Christ, when I read or hear the story of your life on earth, your love for people, your suffering and death for all, my heart is filled with awe and thanksgiving. Coming to your Supper and eating your body and drinking your blood, I find myself going back to that Friday long ago when you gave your life for me and for all the world. Help me never to forget. Amen.

4

The Invitation

Who is invited? There were twelve at the first Supper, twelve followers, one of them about to betray him, one soon to deny him, the others to drift away and be lost in the crowd. To all he gave the bread and wine. He said, "For you."

In Holy Communion God acts to give us the gift of himself, forgiveness and mercy. We who come also act (we eat and drink) to receive him and his blessings. It is as simple as that.

When I stand or kneel before the altar, the words "for you" are in the singular. It is *for me* he suffered and died; it is *for me* that he spreads his table. In that moment I may forget all others, those about me. *I* have been invited. While I am a member of the church, the most royal company on earth, a magnificent fellowship, for an instant I am separated out to face my Lord alone. My importance is just that great.

I come with my own cargo of sin and shortcomings. Others may have a cargo much like mine, but I have no responsibility for theirs, and I cannot hide behind the thought that they are no better, or worse, than I. I stand alone, marooned from my family and crowd. God and I face each other alone. If I say I have no sin, I lie. The wretched things I have done or thought, the good I have neglected to do—all this makes up my cargo. I am there to lay it all out before him. There is no other way for me to accept an invitation from a holy God. To come, as did the Pharisee in Jesus' familiar parable, parading my credentials, I know to be fraudulent. I feel undone before his all-seeing eye. I have no qualifications as a member of my family; there are no credits due me as a member of my profession or the Veterans of Foreign Wars or the labor union. In a profound sense there is great relief in no longer hiding behind anyone or anything, finally to come clean, to be purged of all pretense and shame, to offer myself as a sinner needing mercy.

We would hardly dare to stand defenseless before the high court of God if we had not already learned to know him as a Lord who died for us. We could not unload the cargo, if it were to remain rotting at our feet. We know that in giving his body and blood for us he has made provision to remove the whole festering load as far as the East is from the West.

"He knows our frame; he remembers that we are

dust" (Psalm 103:14). Far better than a mother knows her son or daughter, God knows our needs and weaknesses. Though of eternal worth, every individual is a fragile creature, victim of nameless fears, tempted to envy, pride, suspicion, and despondency. We have fears of inadequacy and rejection. To find meaning and love and hope is a constant struggle. Somewhere death awaits to strike us down. On every step of the way the eye of the Lord is upon us, and in every failure he is there to hold us and lift us.

"Come, my Table is spread for you," says Jesus, "for you who are weak and need me. You need not put your house in order, simply come. I will clear away the debris and give you a new beginning. Only believe, and come."

Holy Communion is for believers, for confessing Christians. It would be quite meaningless for others. Some people, very earnest people, wonder if their faith is good enough or strong enough to qualify them for the Supper. They might very well say, "More than anything, I want to believe. I want it to be true that Christ died for me and that he forgives me, but doubts plague me." I have known people who have denied themselves the blessings of Communion for years because they have misunderstood the nature of faith. Faith never is knowing for sure, like knowing that two plus two equals four, or that Washington, D.C., is the capitol of the U.S.A. Christian faith comes closer to being a wish and a will. "I will to believe that Christ died for me, and that in Holy Communion he gives me his body and blood." Be assured that the will to believe is the work of the Holy Spirit in your heart. Whether you feel a surging certainty or whether your faith is like "a bruised reed," the invitation is for you.

Come to me, all who labor and are heavy laden, and I will give you rest. Take my yoke upon you, and learn from me; for I am gentle and lowly in heart, and you will find rest for your souls. For my yoke is easy, and my burden is light.

Matthew 11:28-30

Draw near and take the body of the Lord
And drink the holy blood for you outpoured.
He who has saints in this world rules and
   shields,
To all believers life eternal yields,
With heavenly bread makes those who hunger
   whole,
Gives living waters to the thirsty soul.
The judge eternal, unto whom shall bow
All nations at the last, is with us now.
   LBW 226

At your invitation I come, O Lord. Take all my sins and, forgiving them, use them to show me the ways of true happiness and the paths of peace. Take me as I am, with my impulses, strivings, and longings so often thwarted, and open for me doors of hope and gladness. Amen.

30

5

Worthy-Unworthy

"I've never had Communion," she informed me. As devout a worker as we had in the Lutheran Student Association at Iowa State University, she had been told by her pastor at the time of her confirmation that unless she gave up her sinful life (dancing, cards, movies), she should not risk "eating and drinking judgment" upon herself, as St. Paul cautions his Corinthian congregation (1 Cor. 11:29). In my early ministry one of the stalwart members of my congregation, member of the church council, never came to the Supper. While on a fishing trip together, he informed me that his mother in Norway had warned him that if he drank beer he would be unworthy and, in Paul's language, would be guilty of "profaning the body and blood of the Lord." While he no longer believed this, he could not bring himself to blemish the memory of his mother by coming. A young pastor at the first Communion service in his new parish was puzzled that only one man, an elderly deacon, came to the altar.

Not only in pietistic and legalistic congregations have Paul's words, "an unworthy manner," or eating and drinking "without discerning the body," been given strange interpretation. On the one hand, worthiness has been interpreted to mean a blameless life, or, on the other hand, a specific doctrinal understanding of the Supper. The Lord may desire both qualities of his followers, but it is doubtful that he would give a test on either score before inviting to the Supper. Still another standard has been that a person should be cld enough to take his or her sinfulness seriously and so be able genuinely to repent.

In an earlier day, when private confession was practiced, when Communion was offered only at special services, and when a person had memorized in confirmation classes the chief doctrines of the church, the question of worthiness and unworthiness was taken seriously. Today when on a Sunday morning the entire congregation, including visitors, is invited to the Lord's Table, the question of "discerning the body" is rarely raised or faced. But the issue is still there.

The moral disorder in the Corinthian congregation was quite different from that of a well-instructed, pious Iowa congregation. There was open adultery, fornication, even incest. Pagan practices were still afflicting the people. When Paul urged them to "examine" themselves, he wasn't cautioning against harmless pleasures. Nor was he probing their doctrinal understanding of Holy Communion. He was lamenting their careless and dissolute lives; he was calling for a change in those lives. He was pleading for dealing with the Supper in the same solemn manner in which it was given by the Lord.

Our manner of life is important to the Lord. We are not to conform to the ways of the world, but to his ways. We are not to be thermometers, merely reflecting the climate of our age; we are to be thermostats, drawing on a transcendent source of power to change the climate of our time. If we do not take discipleship seriously, do we belong to him? To come to Communion as fraudulent followers is to crash the party.

No follower measures up. But if we are earnestly trying, though we fail again and again, and we repent (feel sadness over our sins and shortcomings and desire the Lord's help to do better), the Supper is for us. He is worthy and well prepared, said Luther, who believes these words, "Given and shed for you for the remission of sins." The words, "for you," require truly believing hearts.

To believe, therefore, is the most important credential. Believing is not necessarily a knowledge of all the doctrines that cluster around Holy Communion. Most Christians, asked what they believe, may do little more than confess the Apostles' Creed. To expect them to master the nuances of all the doctrines of the church, desirable as this would be, is to ask far more than the average believer can do. Nor can most of us boast a sublime, untroubled faith. We are disturbed by doubt. But faith never is being utterly sure, like being sure at the mcment that you do sit in a pew and you do eat and drink. Faith is a miracle of the Holy Spirit by which we are moved to reach out to our Lord in gratitude, in response to the wonder of his having died for us.

Most people who say "I don't have enough faith," or "I'm not religious enough," misunderstand the unconditioned invitation of our Lord: "Come to me, all who labor and are heavy laden, and I will give you rest" (Matt. 11:28). We have come to him in Baptism; we come to him in prayer and praise; we come to learn of him every time we open the Bible or hear his Word preached. When he invites us to his Supper, we come to receive again and to be assured again of the endless grace that he offers in giving himself to us. We come with glad and thankful hearts.

Seek the Lord while he may be found, call upon him while he is near; let the wicked forsake his way, and the unrighteous man his thoughts: let him return to the Lord, that he may have mercy on him, and to our God, for he will abundantly pardon. For my thoughts are not your thoughts, neither are your ways my ways, says the Lord. For as the heavens are higher than the earth, so are my ways higher than your ways, and my thoughts than your thoughts.
Isaiah 55:6-9

Amazing grace, how sweet the sound,
That saved a wretch like me!
I once was lost, but now am found;
Was blind, but now I see.

Through many dangers, toils, and snares
I have already come;
'Tis grace has brought me safe thus far,
And grace will lead me home.

The Lord has promised good to me;
His Word my hope secures;
He will my shield and portion be
As long as life endures.
    LBW 448

*I need to look at myself, O Lord, but not too long.
I need to look to you, and to hear your kind invitation to come. My life is a mixture of many things.
At best, my successes in following you may be few;
my need for your continued mercy is great. It is in
confidence that you do not give up on me that I
come. Amen.*

6

Confession

Confession of sin has had a long history in Christian worship. Most Sunday morning services begin with it, and prayers for mercy are a refrain that occurs again and again throughout the worship. It is not peculiar only to the formal worship. It is an integral part of the Christian's life, where in daily renewal we repent, cry for mercy, and affirm our faith.

Nor is private confession to the pastor strange to the Lutheran church. The churches of our immigrant forbears employed it almost without exception. During the week before the three or four Communion services of the year, those who wished to come to the Supper visited the pastor's study at appointed times to "confess" or share with him the issues of their lives that gave them sadness or joy. It was understood that the pastor had the authority to refuse them admission to the Lord's Table if a person's life was at open variance with Christian faith and life. A pastor told me of two brothers who had long had bad blood between them and refused to be reconciled, but, when denied the sacrament, they were brought together in mutual forgiveness.

For many of us, at some time or another, general confession to God in public worship may not be enough to bring peace. The Scriptures encourage us to confess to one another. Where we have wronged someone specifically and a knowing chasm of guilt separates us, it surely is God's will that we reach out to one another, in confession and forgiveness, to bridge the chasm.

One of the most faithful women of my parish called me on Maundy Thursday and asked if I could come to see her. After a Communion service that evening I went. She met me at the door in obvious distress and said, "I'm alone, my husband is in the hospital, and I have been drinking. Do you want to come in?" After I had seated myself, she began deriding the Lutheran Church. (I had not known that she had come from the Roman Catholic Church some years earlier.) "You Lutherans are so stiff you won't even kneel when you pray." After giving vent to her feelings, she became more calm. "You don't have the confessional, and for ten years I haven't felt clean." I asked her if she believed that Lutherans and Catholics worshiped the same God. She said yes. Then, "Do you believe that as a pastor I can hear your confession and give you absolution?" She hesitated a moment, then impulsively came over to my chair, kneeled, and poured out her heart in confession. I placed my hands on her head and spoke the words of absolution. "By the authority of God and my holy office I declare to you the full forgiveness of all your sins in the name of the Father and the Son and the Holy Ghost." Before leaving, I had the feeling that her need for confession had been met and that she could go on in a peace and a strength she had not known for many years.

Many of us may not have any lurid, dramatic sins to confess. At least by the standards of society our sins may seem trivial. By the standards of God, however, they may separate us from him as surely as murder or adultery. Ingratitude, envy, defensiveness, sloth, self-indulgence, indifference, bigotry, impatience—these are qualities that are offensive and intolerable in the kingdom of God. They live in fertile soil among many of us who are in church every Sunday and pay regularly our cautious pledge to the organized work of the church. When in the general prayer of confession we say, "We have not loved you with our whole heart; we have not loved our neighbors as ourselves," not a single one of us can stand before God as a trivial sinner. Our self-concern and self-interest are so deep that we are totally unfit for life with our crucified Lord. We have no option but to cry for mercy, and hope that there is mercy, even for us.

We live in a day when psychologists are telling us to express everything. Unfortunately, most of them, unless they understand the elemental need of expressing everything *to God*, do very little but confuse catharsis with forgiveness. The cargo you have left exposed must have a place of disposal. It will not go away simply by letting it see the light of day. Then it only rots on the outside instead of on the inside. Confession and forgiveness belong together.

Nor is it enough to confess in order to be forgiven by another. The psychiatrist cannot forgive; he is not the wronged one; you did him no harm. The person you have wronged may not be able to forgive, or may not want to. The wrong is basically against the God who gives us life and who redeems it. Horizontal confession is not enough. We live in a vertical world —God and I. When David the king had committed adultery with Bathsheba, and had arranged her husband Uriah's death, in his deep guilt David cried to God, "Against thee, thee only, have I sinned" (Ps. 51:4). He could not make amends to Bathsheba by divorcing her or abandoning her; he could not make it up to the murdered Uriah. The cargo of his sin, once exposed, could be confessed and disposed of with God alone.

Sin is not a word taken very seriously in our day. We have slipped into the fraudulent fashion of measuring our lives not against Jesus but against our contemporaries. We have abandoned the hard, concrete laws of integrity, purity, and love, and have surrendered to the mores of society. To break the promise made in marriage and drift to the divorce court can't be too wicked, we think, because many people do it. To cheat on our taxes is a trifle; who doesn't? To forget the Sixth Commandment and co-habit without marriage and commitment can't be that sinful since my friends take it for granted. The whole orientation is as phony as the boy who tells his dad, "Dad, it's O.K. Everybody's doing it." If the whole fabric of society is not to crumble, we will need again to establish the laws of God as the standard. Any other standard will bring anarchy.

Flanking us at the Table are people whose lives are perhaps no better or worse than ours. We may be tempted to measure ourselves by them. But it is the Lord we face, and measured by him we have no option but to plead for mercy. And there is mercy.

When I declared not my sin, my body wasted away through my groaning all day long. For day and night thy hand was heavy upon me; my strength was dried up as by the heat of summer. I acknowledged my sin to thee, and I did not hide my iniquity; I said, "I will confess my transgressions to the Lord"; then thou didst forgive the guilt of my sin.

Psalm 32:3-5

Just as I am, without one plea,
But that thy blood was shed for me,
And that thou bidst me come to thee,
O Lamb of God, I come, I come.
Just as I am, though tossed about
With many a conflict, many a doubt,
Fightings and fears within, without,

O Lamb of God, I come, I come.
Just as I am, thou wilt receive,
Wilt welcome, pardon, cleanse, relieve;
Because thy promise I believe,
O Lamb of God, I come, I come.
      LBW 296

*That you will receive us as we are without any pre-
liminaries is one of your wonders, O Lord. We know,
however, that to come into your presence means to
drop all pretense and any defense we have had. Your
all-seeing eye looks through us. We confess to you
that we have no credentials of holiness. We have
sinned and are sinful human beings. Upon your invitation and with no strings attached, we come to receive your comfort and to be reinvolved with all your
enterprises on earth. Help us not to retreat from full
discipleship. Amen.*

7

The Common Stuff

Why would God knit the profound "spiritual" truths to some very simple physical things like water (in Baptism) and bread and wine (in Communion)? This would have been intolerable for the ancient Greeks who neatly separated the physical from the spiritual, and even regarded the spiritual as good and the physical as bad. But the God who created us body and soul and said it was good is not a Greek philosopher.

Still, it is a puzzle, even for Christians. Why did Christ institute sacraments, and why should the sacrament of Baptism and the sacrament of Holy Communion occupy such a central place in the life of the church? Is not his Word enough?

During these few swift years on earth we inhabit a body that eats and drinks, needs clothing and shelter, reproduces its kind, knows pain and pleasure. Our bodies are very much with us and are interlocked with our spirits. Our spirits are lifted by good food and drink; they relax into serenity before a flaming fireplace; they glow at the touch of the beloved's hand or lips. If my granddaughter, at the other end of the room, says, "Grandpa, I love you," that's one thing; if she comes running, flings her arms about me, and whispers, "Grandpa, I love you," that's another thing. The assurance of her love is reinforced by the physical. Her word of love reaches my heart, in part, through my body.

How would an ascended Lord, among us still but invisible, reinforce his Word of love? How would he penetrate the physical, throw his arms around us? Through water and bread and wine. Nor are these only lessons or demonstrations. The arms of my granddaughter are not mere exhibits; they carry her love, they are love. The bread and wine are not only *reminders* of his presence and love; they *are* his presence and love.

The body and soul are both creations of God. Human disobedience separates both from the life of God. When Christ died to reconcile humankind to God and to bridge the chasm between them, he died for the whole person, body and soul. When, upon death, God raises us up to everlasting life, he raises the whole person, body and soul, to live with him. Heaven is for both souls *and bodies*, bodies now glorified and imperishable as the Lord's. Strangely enough, this prospect is often alien to the Christian who still lives with the Greek mythology of heaven inhabited by disembodied spirits, like wisps of vapor.

A few Christian groups, very few, have repudiated sacraments as not central to the Christian faith, or even as a distraction. The Quakers, for instance, who with high moral purpose follow the teachings of Jesus, have excluded the sacraments from their worship for fear that one might get lost in outward rites and be detoured from the exalted and stern command to love one another. A postwar Christian group in Japan, committed to Christ's teaching of purity and love, has also excluded the sacraments, for fear of being regarded as only another religion of meaningless ceremonies. Within the large Christian family, there are many people who, though deeply loyal to Christ, have never found either Baptism or Holy Communion especially edifying. The profound connection between the spiritual and the physical has not penetrated the meaning of the sacramental for them. It has been difficult for me.

Long ago, as I wrestled with this question, it occurred to me that the Lord may have instituted the sacraments largely to reassure me of his love. The parallel of a promissory note helped me. My friend, for instance, tells me that on a given date he will pay me $1000. I trust him and say, "Your word is good enough for me." But he insists on putting his word into writing. He takes the common stuff of ink and paper and "in, with, and under" these purely physical elements (stuff that I can see and hold in my hand) he writes the words of promise. I may still protest, but he insists on giving me his written, promissory note to anchor my trust in something concrete. Without presuming to read the mind of the Lord, I have been comforted by this parallel.

It has also been meaningful to me that the Lord chose the most common stuff of earth—water, bread, wine—instead of some rare and exotic material. Somehow he has exalted the ordinary things easily available and useful to everyone in the everyday needs of life. These, which nourish the body and give it life, now are made the means that nourish and give life to the soul.

For as the rain and the snow come down from heaven, and return not thither but water the earth, making it bring forth and sprout, giving seed to the sower and bread to the eater, so shall my word be that goes forth from my mouth; it shall not return to me empty, but it shall accomplish that which I purpose, and prosper in the thing for which I sent it.

Isaiah 55:10-11

O Bread of life from heaven,
O Food to pilgrims given,
O Manna from above:
Feed with the blessed sweetness
Of your divine completeness
The souls that want and need your love.
LBW 222

O Lord, in your wisdom you have given us bodies and

placed us on this earth, lavishingly providing for our daily needs. We thank you that all things seen and touched can speak of your goodness. Help us not to take these gifts for granted, but that in and through them all we touch your mercies. As we come to your Supper and taste the bread and wine, transport us beyond the world of the seen into the world of the unseen, to know that we are in your eternal care. Amen.

8

Eucharist

Sadness has often been the tone of Holy Communion. It *is* a solemn service, but so is a wedding, a baptism, confirmation. Solemnity is not necessarily sadness, but can be deep joy and thanksgiving. In the past, Communion concentrated so much on repentance that we rarely made the turn to exultation over forgiveness and restoration.

In the liturgies of Communion there is an attempt to dislodge us from guilt and fear to a glad thanksgiving for God's immeasurable grace. We are his people, his sons and daughters, invited to his Table. Here he gives us himself for the forgiveness of sins, to be sure, but he does this whenever and however he comes. Forgiveness is but a door; it is not the palace, it is not the kingdom. As far as the East is from the West, so far does he remove our sins. He remembers them no more and he invites us, having been forgiven, to stride boldly into the riches of his kingdom where there is singing and dancing and merriment forevermore.

We come to the Table in repentance, of course, but don't we come to him always as unworthy children? It is in and through the gracious work of Christ's atonement that we dare to come at all. He receives us, forgives us, and ushers us into his jubilant presence. This he does whenever we hear or read or remember the glad, good news of his gospel. Our coming to the Lord's Supper is no special kind of coming.

Holy Communion is often called the *Eucharist,* which means thanksgiving. Even when we approach him with our sins, we come in faith that he waits to forgive. We know that even before we hear the words, "Your sins are forgiven." We don't tremble in fear that he may withhold his mercy. We know that his arms are open to receive us.

Gratitude is a dominant note in the whole of the Christian life. We thank him for all good; we blame him for no evil. This may not be consistent, but it is the way of the Christian. And what a long inventory of blessings we have in the common, repetitious gifts of sunshine and rain, food and clothing, friends and family, country and government, church and school. There is nothing in our lives that cannot inspire us to gratitude. Even when we encounter adversity and illness, we thank him that he is in the midst of our lives, to sorrow with us and to give us strength to endure.

A thankful heart starts with God's supreme love in sending his only Son to die for us. Knowing that God receives us as we are, restores us to full rights in the kingdom, and assures us of an everlasting place with him in heaven, we find evidences of his goodness everywhere. For us who have found God's love at the cross, everything—the birds that sing, the laughter of a child, the stars that shine, the touch of the beloved's hand—everything speaks of the love of our heavenly Father.

It may be possible for a person to be thankful, to have a general mood of contentment, without being thankful *to* anyone in particular. But normally a person who is thankful *for* something, wants to be thankful *to someone.* Long ago I read a poem entitled, "The Atheist's Wail," which in essence said: I can writhe on a bed of pain and steel myself, and I don't need God. I can stand at the open grave of a loved one and steel myself, and I don't need God. But when the sun is shining brightly and the autumn trees are in full color, and I'm walking through the woods with my beloved's hand in mine, it's a terrible thing not to have anyone to thank.

A gift is not a reward; there's a great difference. A reward is in payment for something, for some achievement, some work well done. You *deserve* reward. You may be pleased to receive it, but you need not be thankful. You have earned it. If God's favor is given you because you have done well, or because you have such sublime faith, or because you have had a striking religious experience, then his grace is reward and will generate no gratitude. More likely, you may grow proud, self-righteous, even haughty. You make God your debtor, you his creditor; he owes you. God refuses to be a debtor; he gives all.

He *is* pleased to have you; he paid a great price for you. During a slave auction a man bought a fine young man, and gave him his freedom. Overwhelmed, the young man asked if he couldn't still be his man and serve him. In some such way we respond to the incredible good news that we have been redeemed from sin and evil with no strings attached. Our life with God is a gift, a pure gift. And the response to a gift is gratitude. "What language shall I borrow to thank thee, dearest friend?" is the cry of every Christian.

He gives us a language. It is the language of service. As our Lord became a servant, we are to be servants. As the Lord allowed all people to have a claim on him, we are to allow all people's needs and wants to reach us. We give ourselves to him, and he gives us to the world. Over the exit door of a church there is a simple inscription, "Servant's Entrance." As people leave the service and the Lord's Table, and their hearts beat with gratitude, they are reminded that they are now dedicated to the needs of the world.

I appeal to you therefore, brethren, by the mercies of God, to present your bodies as a living sacrifice, holy and acceptable to God, which is your spiritual worship. Do not be conformed to this world but be transformed by the renewal of your mind, that you may prove what is the will of God, what is good and acceptable and perfect.

Romans 12:1-2

Now thank we all our God with hearts and
    hands and voices,
Who wondrous things has done, in whom his
    world rejoices;
Who, from our mothers' arms has blest us
    on our way
With countless gifts of love, and still is ours
    today.

Oh, may this bounteous God through all our
    life be near us,
With ever joyful hearts and blessed peace
    to cheer us,
And keep us in his grace, and guide us when
    perplexed,
And free us from all harm in this world and
    the next.

All praise and thanks to God the Father now
    be given,
The Son, and him who reigns with them in
    highest heaven,

The one eternal God, whom earth and heaven
   adore;
For thus it was, is now, and shall be evermore.
   LBW 533

*Help us, O Lord, to sing for joy as we leave your
Table, to leave our "low-vaulted past" of sin and
shame and fear, to walk unafraid into your presence,
and to face bravely the work you have for us in your
world. Give us grace to thank you as long as we live,
in days of prosperity and adversity, health and sick-
ness. To us you have given the greatest gift of all—
yourself. Amen.*

9

Communion

We are created for fellowship. "It is not good that the man should be alone," said God, and created a companion for Adam. We may be called gregarious, social creatures, or whatever; the truth is that we are born into a company, the human race, whether we like it or not, and at Baptism we are reborn into another company, the Holy Christian Church. No one has the option of being alone, not even alone with God. There are no private parties in heaven. A person may try to make it on their own, but any boast of having done so is stark falsehood. We may be egocentric enough to try, but it won't work.

It is not by chance that the Lord's Supper has been called Holy Communion—communion with God and communion with one another. Only at one place do we stand alone before God: at the moment of judgment we are separated from all others. There we cannot be lost in the crowd; there we cannot plead credit through a devout mother; there we cannot beg extenuating circumstances because of a negligent father. We stand quite alone to be judged. But the moment of forgiveness flings the doors of the kingdom wide open, and a vast company awaits us.

The company includes not only those who belong to our church, not to the followers of Christ alone, but the whole human race for whom our Lord died and whom he gives us as neighbors. Let no one think that he belongs only to that "little flock whom Jesus calls his own." Belonging to Christ is not a cozy affair. There is one God, the Father of all. It may not be pleasant to claim the atheist, the Communist, the Buddhist, or your grumpy neighbor. But the circle is wide enough to include them all. By being Christian I am restored to the whole human race, and not simply because I have learned to like them. Shylock the Jew in Shakespeare's *The Merchant of Venice,* pleads, "When you prick us, do we not bleed?" It is not that both the Jew and I bleed that brings us together. It is that our God is God of all, and we belong to his big family, the human race.

Within the big circle there are smaller ones. Country, family, race, creeds form orbits which God himself honors and loves. Just as he once singled out Abraham and his family for a special mission in his plan, so he has now established a new family, a new colony on earth, the one, holy, Christian, and apostolic church. These are the people who have been brought into intimate fellowship with him through faith in his Son. The fellowship that belongs to this company is deeper and more abiding than any other on earth. We are one with him as the several branches are one in the tree trunk through which they have life. We are the restored members of his greater family.

Many yet remain to be drawn in. We dare not boast, but by grace we are the elect, the royal priesthood, the heirs of the kingdom. That God loves us more than those yet outside is not true. He loves all his children equally, those who are outside and those inside, his lost son in the far country and his son at home. We have been brought home by grace through faith. Our deepest fellowship is within that home.

Even in human terms, fellowship around a meal is a singularly warm fellowship. The fellowship of the Lord's Supper is that kind, and more. The first Supper in the secret room must have been memorable for Jesus and the twelve. He told them that this was the last time he would eat with them until he had come into his kingdom. It was after they had eaten that he made the meal truly unique. He took bread and wine and said, "Eat, drink. This is my body and my blood."

Loneliness is always painful. For many people in our urban society, the tragedy of existence is being marooned into a forgotten anonymity, even more than early immigrants in the sparsely settled prairies or woods. Loneliness is not measured in numbers alone. On the prairies neighbors could be miles apart, but they cared for one another. Today, lost in teeming tenements or in isolated "high-rise cells," forgotten or ignored by family and friends, people cry out for companionship. While a distraction from their boredom, radio and television cannot take away the dull ache of being forgotten. Only fellowship with living, caring human beings can bring warmth and meaning.

Communion with God, basic as that is, cannot fill the void for most people. We don't have the inner resources of the Desert Fathers. God himself doesn't want us to settle for a life with him alone. He made us for each other, to care for one another. If there is no caring, there is no fellowship. A bus depot, with hundreds of people hurrying by, can be as lonely a place as a desert. If one person, an old friend, stops by to greet you, the depot glows with warmth.

When we call the Supper *Holy Communion* we are not dealing only in mystery. This is the coming together of a family, a family that is loved by their one Father, is served by their one Lord, and lives by the one indwelling Spirit. It is a family that has learned to know one another, has rejoiced and grieved together, as pilgrims together on the way to their eternal home. Each one is unique; no two are alike. We differ in tastes, in occupation, in levels of wealth and station, in political convictions, perhaps in race. But we are one in the profoundest unity on earth. If anyone fails to find fellowship in the Christian congregation, it is probably because they have not tried seriously to find it. Seated beside me on a flight, a man said, "In my business I'm occasionally transferred to a new city. The very first thing our family does is to find a church home. There is no place in society where a person or family can find such good friends, such support, as in a congregation, and we need that."

As we approach the Table we may be flanked by people yet strangers. But they are our brothers and sisters in the Lord. Receiving the Lord's body and blood, we remember that we are grafted into him, each of us, and that in him we are no longer lonely, isolated cells, but we are one with all others who also eat and drink with us.

For just as the body is one and has many members, and all the members of the body, though many, are one body, so it is with Christ. For by one Spirit we were all baptized into one body—Jews or Greeks, slaves or free—and all are made to drink of one Spirit. . . . If one member suffers, all suffer together; if one member is honored, all rejoice together. Now you are the body of Christ and individually members of it.

1 Cor. 12:12-13; 26-27

Lord Jesus Christ, we humbly pray
That we may feast on thee today;
Beneath these forms of bread and wine
Enrich us with thy grace divine.

One bread, one cup, one body, we,
United by our life in thee,
Thy love proclaim till thou shalt come
To bring thy scattered loved ones home.
LBW 225

*Grant, O God, that because we meet together here
this morning, life may grow greater for some who
have contempt for it, simpler for some who are con-
fused by it, happier for some who are tasting the bit-
terness of it, safer for some who are feeling the peril
of it, more friendly for some who are feeling the
loneliness of it, serener for some who are throbbing
with the fever of it, holier for some to whom life
has lost all dignity, beauty and meaning. Through
Jesus Christ our Lord. Amen.*

(Source Unknown)

10

With Hosts

There is no point in the Communion service that so effectively vaults me into the company that awaits me on the other side of death as when the pastor prays, "And so, with the church on earth and the hosts of heaven, we praise your name and join their unending hymn." It is as if I join them in the feast of victory where the Lord himself "shall come and serve them." He serves me the Supper here; he serves them there.

The church on earth is impoverished if it is not constantly aware of its counterpart in heaven. We are pilgrims here, but heaven is our home. A few short years and our pilgrimage here is over. We go to join the great host in the mansions the Lord has prepared for us.

Many Protestant churches do little to remind their

people of this company. Saints days are largely ignored. The Roman and the Eastern churches have done more to keep alive the reality of the church triumphant. If a child is born on a saint's day, he or she may receive the name of that saint. Whatever abuses may have come from the accent on saints, the church has been enriched by an awareness of the larger family.

When our son was killed, there was no scripture that so lifted my spirits as that magnificent picture of the "cloud of witnesses" in Hebrew 12. I pictured Paul in a vast cheering section, encouraging me to lay aside the weight of grief and return with zest to the joys and tasks of our common life. We who are still running the race of life need the support not only of our fellow runners but also of those whose race is over and who have been awarded the victor's prize.

It is a pardonable oversight that we become so absorbed in our life here that we spend little time pondering heaven. After all, it is here and now, on this earth, that we have our tasks, tasks of the kingdom. Like the quiet stirrings of the sea, however, yearnings and longings that earth cannot satisfy keep murmuring that we are on our way to a better country.

The literature of every culture and religion speaks poignantly, often fearfully, of death and what lies beyond. It is the character of the Christian to face death with expectation and hope in knowing that a heavenly company and a heavenly home await us there. Life on this side is precious since this island too is the Lord's, but it is the mainland that is our real home. When, one by one, our dear ones die, we become increasingly aware of those who have been raised with Christ to the ultimate newness of life and who await our coming.

As we come together at the Lord's Table, it is well to remember that someone now at our side, may, before we meet again, have made the long journey. This should make the moment more precious, the present relationship we have with each other more dear. How often, when someone has dropped out of the ranks here, do we not regret having treated one another so casually? We might have spoken the encouraging word and didn't. Fortunately, death is not the sad end. There is another time of feasting and communing, and this time the Lord will be our visible host.

Though invisible now in bread and wine, he is here. He is not exiled at the right hand of the Father alone. His presence is not restricted to the limited and capricious capacities of our hearts only. He is here at the Table, as he said: This is my body; this is my blood.

These all died in faith, not having received what was promised, but having seen it and greeted it from afar, and having acknowledged that they were strangers and exiles on the earth . . . . they desire a better country, that is, a heavenly one. Therefore God is not ashamed to be called their God, for he has pre-

pared for them a city. . . . Therefore, since we are surrounded by so great a cloud of witnesses, let us lay aside every weight, and sin which clings so closely, and let us run with perseverance the race that is set before us, looking to Jesus the pioneer and perfecter of our faith.

Hebrews 11:13, 16; 12:1-2

For all the saints who from their labors rest,
All who by faith before the world confessed,
Your name, O Jesus, be forever blest. Alleluia!

From earth's wide bounds, from ocean's farthest
   coast,
Through gates of pearl streams in the countless
   host,
Singing to Father, Son and Holy Ghost:
   Alleluia!

The golden evening brightens in the west:
Soon, soon to faithful warriors comes their rest;
Sweet is the calm of paradise the blest. Alleluia!
   LBW 174

"Out of sight, out of mind" is not true, O Lord. As one by one of my family and friends die and join you on the other side, they are often in my mind more than when they were in the next city. Does this mean, O Lord, that they are more real now than when they were here? I am glad that my faith gives me a right to think that they are cheering me on

and that when death comes for me, I will not be plunged into the abyss but will join them and you in that great cloud of witnesses. Thank you for dying to assure me of this. Amen.

11

Change

The changeless is a strong motif in all religions. The Christian faith is no exception. We confess Jesus, the same yesterday, today, and forever. We sing, "Change and decay in all around I see: O Thou who changest not, abide with me." Our book, the Bible, was finished many centuries ago. Even new cults don't want to be new; they try to anchor their beliefs and practices in the ancient past, the more ancient the better. No one really wants a new religion.

Practices do change; architecture changes; new hymns and new liturgies appear. Within these changes the faith remains constant. We may resist change even in practices, architecture, and forms of service. We are edified by the familiar. C. S. Lewis speaks for many Christians when he said that he too was in favor of change: one word every hundred years. When the immigrant churches had to shift from the Scandinavian or German languages to the English, our forebears had their troubles. My grandfather could trade horses in his faltering English; he would pray only in his native Norwegian. I too have my troubles. When today a new book of worship trips me up with changes in the wording of creeds or the Lord's Prayer, or thrusts a new hymn at me, I squirm. Quickly I remind myself of the psalmist's words, "Praise him with a new song," and make a serious try at the new melody. The next hymn, an old favorite, saves the day for me.

The Lord's Supper has not changed since the twelve sat with their Master, but the manner of observance has. In my South Dakota youth the service was an unhurried affair. Communion was preceded by the service of confession; we were ushered to the altar to kneel and have the pastor declare the absolution with the laying on of hands, one by one. We came to the altar a second time to receive the bread and wine. I miss the words of absolution addressed directly to me with the touch of the pastor's hand on my brow. I miss the leisurely tempo. During my 20 years as a pastor Communion was always a separate service, usually in the late afternoon or early evening, never at the morning service. We never had to hurry.

Only those who had completed their confirmation instruction were invited to come. Children were never seen at the altar. Today whole families of all ages come, and Holy Communion is served to communicants who may not be confirmed for still many years. Kneelers at the altar were a standard fixture in all churches; seldom did one receive the sacrament while standing. I lived through the transition from the common cup to individual glasses, and now, in many churches, back to the common cup and the one loaf.

Many of these changes have come largely from practical necessity, some of them from a desire to return to symbols of the earlier church. The more frequent observances of today, and the inclusion of the whole congregation, doubtless reflect an attempt to give the Supper more inclusive participation. Try as we will, it is doubtful that several hundred people moving up and down the aisles of a big church can recapture the warmth and solemnity of a small band of persecuted Christians gathered in some secret retreat. It will take devout and disciplined minds to keep the Supper from being casual and routine.

Until recently only an ordained pastor could celebrate Holy Communion and distribute the elements. In most instances the pastor did not commune himself, with the result that he was never a part of the communing congregation, and shared the Supper only at pastors' conferences. The renewed awareness of the priesthood of all believers, one of the great Reformation rediscoveries, has opened the door to lay people assisting and communing the pastor.

The mood of Holy Communion has changed from an atmosphere of sorrow over sin to thanksgiving for grace. Both motifs are valid. Many of us who grew up in the somber days have fears that sin, repentance, and the deep need for pardon are bypassed and that, in consequence, the real source of joy and celebration will be lost too. Professor Herman A. Preus, long a pastor and theological professor, reflects this uneasiness, "When Holy Communion was celebrated only a few times a year, I recall the communion eve when my father would take our family to the pastor's sacristy for private confession. Family prayers that evening also were a part of the preparation for the solemn and festive celebration the next day. . . . Have we lost some of this reverence?"

I am quite willing to concede that the new note of joy is a gain. In former times we never quite escaped from the heaviness of sin and guilt into gladness. After all, we should have remembered that, as children of God, we were already reconciled and could come to be reminded of a grace that had clasped us from the hour of our Baptism. Reverence can be expressed by joy as well as by sorrow.

When changes come, as they have and will—whether dictated by new circumstances, whether by the Spirit leading us into new dimensions of the truth, or whether by returning to lost riches of the past—it is our privilege to be open to the Giver of all grace, who doesn't change and who can bless us in a variety of forms.

Lord, thou hast been our dwelling place in all generations. Before the mountains were brought forth, or ever thou hadst formed the earth and the world, from everlasting to everlasting thou art God. Thou turnest man back to the dust, and sayest, "Turn back, O children of men!" For a thousand years in thy sight are but as yesterday when it is past, or a watch in the night. Psalm 90:1-4

O God, our help in ages past,
Our hope for years to come,
Our shelter from the stormy blast,
And our eternal home:

Under the shadow of your throne
Your saints have dwelt secure;
Sufficient is your arm alone,
And our defense is sure.

Before the hills in order stood
Or earth received its frame,
From everlasting you are God,
To endless years the same.
LBW 320

O Lord, you know how we cherish the familiar and are suspicious of something new. We thank you that you do not change and that your promises are sure. Keep us from being so fastened to the past that we cannot see either the usefulness or the inspiration of change. Whatever else in the service may be different, the words you spoke to your disciples at the first Supper—"This is my body . . . this is my blood"—are the words you now speak to me. For this I give you thanks. Amen.

12

Beyond Words

Worship is hearing and speaking; worship is also acting, by doing. Deeds are more enduring than words.

Rabbi Lionel Blue, in his book, *The Jewish Path to God,* says, "Language is good when it talks about objects like pots and pans; it stammers when it tries to communicate deeper experience, such as great love; it is inadequate when it tries to tell about such things as a meeting with infinity, or appointment with destiny."

Upon hearing the words, "This is my body . . . this is my blood," you *do* something: you eat and drink. This is but the climax of a whole series of acts that led up to this moment. You began the ritual of *doing* when you resisted the impulse to sleep in, and dressed and went to church. You entered the pew, you arose for the reading of Scripture and prayer. You walked to the altar, you may have knelt, you ate and drank. Perhaps you made the sign of the cross, as Luther advised. Somewhere in the service you made your offering of money. To be sure, you heard words and you spoke and sang words, perhaps without much thought. But from the moment you awakened until you returned home, by what you did you performed the rituals of obedience and reverence.

The Christian church is less ritualistic than the Jewish church; the Lutheran churches less than the Roman Catholic or Eastern churches; for the most part other Protestant churches less than the Lutheran. In fact, some parts of Christendom have spurned repetitious ritual as pagan. In so doing, they have ignored human nature and have robbed God of mystery and awe. They threaten to reduce religion to an idea or to a philosophy. Theologians of all churches, their business being words, have at times denied themselves the wonder of the unknown and unknowable by presuming to package truth and God into neat propositions or rhetoric. People untutored in words have sometimes, through symbols and deeds, drawn nearer to the infinite than their more learned brothers and sisters.

The love of country, for instance, is not a matter primarily for words. The emotions that surge when we sing "The Star-Spangled Banner" or "America the Beautiful" would be little evidence of love if a person refused the "ritual" of serving and defending the land, or eluded the "ritual" of paying taxes, or ignored the disciplines of caring for the resources of the land. If the language of deeds is not there, the love of country is not there.

What is it that endears a person to family? Recollection of words, words of love and encouragement? Perhaps. But words are important only as they are woven into a whole fabric of deeds—a mother's unflagging provision of food and clothing for her family, father's sitting at a child's bedside all through a night of illness. Birthdays, holidays, and Christmas generate customs which now the children, with children of their own, transmit to the next generation as loving, cohesive traditions. What they *said* may long since have been forgotten, but not what they *did*.

Let no one say that to eat and drink bread and wine, again and again, is hollow ritual. "This *do*," he commanded, and we *do*. Holy Communion is a means of grace. God breaks through and embraces his child in strange and unexpected ways. A friend of mine told of his conversion. He had fallen away from the faith. But one Sunday, after long absence from church, lonely and in a strange city, he wandered into the service. Not quite knowing why, he came to the altar for Holy Communion. And then it happened—through the simple words and the simple act of eating and drinking. He said, "I left the table a new man, forgiven, and restored to my God." There was no oratory, no emotion-filled altar call, no pressure from the crowd. Through the sacrament, God stole into his heart.

Even laying aside the Sunday paper and dressing

for church is in a strange way sacramental. You *do*. And doing is worship. To sit quietly and meditate is worship; to read the Scriptures is worship; to listen to the sermon is worship. But Christ says little about meditation; the Gospels are filled with his exhortation to do. "Every one then who hears these words of mine and does them . . ." he said.

What we do in the hour of worship is but a clue to the whole of the Christian life—an obedient and grateful response to what God has done and is doing for us. We thank him and we praise him. We adore him. We do this by what we say and do in worship. But it is after the hour of worship—after the Communion that a life of deeds unfolds. To thank him in truth is to become his servants, slaves in fact, and as slaves he sells us to the world. Just as he emptied himself of his royal station and took the form of a slave to the needs and wants of the world, he enlists us in the same grand enterprise. To find and do his will becomes the goal of life. All other goals, even security and survival, are swallowed up in this one towering purpose. And his will for us is to serve the neighbor—all people everywhere.

Not everyone who says to me, "Lord, Lord," shall enter the kingdom of heaven, but he who does the will of my Father who is in heaven. On that day many will say to me, "Lord, Lord, did we not prophesy in your name, and cast out demons in your name, and do mighty works in your name?" And then will

I declare to them, "I never knew you; depart from me, you evildoers."   Matthew 7:21-23

"Come, follow me," the Savior spake,
"All in my way abiding;
Deny yourselves, the world forsake,
Obey my call and guiding.
Oh, bear the cross, whate'er betide;
Take my example for your guide.

"I am the light; I light the way,
A godly life displaying;
I bid you walk as in the day;
I keep your feet from straying.
I am the way, and well I show
How you should sojourn here below."
    LBW 455

Teach me, O Lord, that a kind deed is more eloquent than a sweet word. Even in worship, let me not ignore or minimize the little things I do in obedience to you. I did get dressed; I did walk into your house; I did eat and drink your body and blood. This simple sequence of events I may have done without speaking a word in worship. But I did it all at your invitation, and I count on your blessings. Amen.

13

The Sermon

In the great reforms of the 16th century, the sermon was restored as the central part of the service. It had been replaced and lost in a multiplicity of rites and ceremonies presided over by an authoritarian priesthood. The people, largely unlearned, were taught to go through the motions of rituals, but were largely left in the dark about the rich treasures of the Scriptures. Luther and the reformers brought the church back to teaching and preaching the Word. In the long history of Christendom, whenever ritual and liturgy and ceremonies have elbowed out the sermon, the evangelical zeal of the church has been in jeopardy.

We are taught that the Holy Spirit uses the means of grace—the Word of God, Baptism, and Holy Communion—to do his work in the human heart. The water in Baptism and the bread and wine in Communion would be quite meaningless without the Word of God, his promises. In order for people to understand in the simplest and most rudimentary way what the sacraments are about, they must have been taught from the Word of God.

The Christian pulpit both teaches and exhorts. Teaching occurs in many of the activities of the congregation (Sunday school, confirmation classes, parish education), of course, but it is on Sunday morning that pastors have the singular opportunity of teaching the Word. If they neglect this opportunity and give only ethical lectures, however much they enliven their talk with illustrations and stories, they betray the purpose of the sermon. They are called to teach the Scriptures and apply them to the lives of people.

To say of your pastor, "He has such a mellow, pleasing voice; his pulpit presence is so commanding; his stories are so interesting," may be no tribute at all. These qualities describe the art of the orator; they say nothing about the substance of the sermon. "Does he preach faithfully the Word of God, disquieting as that may be for us sinners?" This is the test.

Unlike the sacraments, the sermon tempts preachers to intrude their own personalities, for good or ill. In Holy Communion they fade away, as it were. They read the words of institution; they give you the bread and wine. Here they function as the clear agents of God.

While preachers' personal gifts, certainly their zeal, cannot be separated from the sermon, one should be able to say, "It was the Word of God that reached me today; it was as if the preacher was an ambassador, transmitting to me the Word she had received from Another." It is only then that the Word comes alive, and penetrates as a "two-edged sword."

Today the sermon again is threatened. If a full liturgy, with the proper number of hymns and the serving of several hundred people at Communion, must be squeezed into one hour, the sermon may become the casualty. In our immigrant churches the sermon normally was a careful exposition of the biblical text and was rarely less than an hour in length. A pastor in a pioneer Illinois church often preached more than three hours. When the congregation voted that the sermon should not be over three hours long, he protested that there were some texts he could not possibly cover in three hours. Whereupon the congregation reconsidered its action, and voted that when he came to such a text, at the end of three hours they would recess and come back for the rest of the sermon. Where today there are two or three services on a Sunday morning, obviously this Illinois pastor could not be accommodated. But every congregation should be vigilant to allow for a substantial time for the sermon, even if it means curtailing parts of the liturgy.

Both the Word and the sacraments are means of grace, to be sure, and it may be improper to compare their importance in God's plan. In the sheer matter of time allotted to each in the church's ministry, the teaching and preaching of the Word obviously is the leader. In the matter of significance in the life of the believer, a division of time may be no measure. In recent years at Luther Northwestern Seminary, for instance, where we meet five times a week for worship, it is on Wednesday when we have Holy Communion that attendance is at its height. The Lord's Supper clearly ministers to the students' needs.

Whether in preaching or in the sacraments, it is the Word of God that carries the freight. Without that Word neither preaching nor the sacraments have any significance.

For, "everyone who calls on the name of the Lord will be saved." But how are men to call upon him in whom they have not believed? And how are they to believe in him of whom they have never heard? And how are they to hear without a preacher? And how can men preach unless they are sent? As it is written, "How beautiful are the feet of those who preach good news!" But they have not all heeded the gospel; for Isaiah says, "Lord, who has believed what he has heard from us?" So faith comes from what is heard, and what is heard comes by the preaching of Christ. Romans 10:13-17

How firm a foundation, O saints of the Lord,
Is laid for your faith in his excellent Word!
What more can he say than to you he has said
Who unto the Savior for refuge have fled?

Fear not, I am with you, oh, be not dismayed,
For I am your God and will still give you aid;
I'll strengthen you, help you, and cause you to
    stand,
Upheld by my righteous, omnipotent hand.

Throughout all their lifetime my people shall
    prove
My sovereign, eternal, unchangeable love;
And then, when gray hairs shall their temples
    adorn,
Like lambs they shall still in my bosom be borne.
    LBW 507

Help us, O Lord, to rely on your Word with childlike trust. When we hear the gracious words, "Your sins are forgiven," give us the comfort of resting back into your assurance, as children in the arms of a parent. Amen.

14

Without Ears

If you were deaf, and in a church service heard nothing, you would still be surrounded by all sorts of messages about God and from God. The messages would reach you before you entered the church doors. Approaching the church, your eye would catch sight of a church steeple, a finger pointing you upward to God and heaven, or you would see a tower, like a fortress, telling you of the strength and permanence of God. Again and again the symbol of the cross will meet you, reminding you that it was Christ's death that made it possible for us to be forgiven and to be restored children of God.

Only occasionally in a Lutheran church will you see a crucifix, a cross with the form of Jesus suspended, calling you back to those hours of Friday's crucifixion. If you remember your Bible well enough, you may recall some or all of the seven last words that Jesus spoke from the cross, perhaps most clearly his "Father, forgive them for they know not what they do," the word of great comfort for all of us. It is the empty cross you most likely will see in most of our churches, the cross of victory—his suffering over, his work done, humanity restored to the Father. Throughout the service, too, the sign of the cross will be made by the pastor, perhaps by you and others as you receive the bread and wine.

In most of our churches, you will be seated in pews that focus your eyes toward the chancel, the elevated area where the high altar may help you to think of the Lord "high and lifted up," as in Isaiah's vision, Christ seated now at the right hand of the Father in power. More recently many churches have been built almost oval or square, with the pews in a semicircle, family style, the ornate, marble altar replaced by a table. This design emphasizes the Lord in the midst of his people, as the shepherd with his flock. Sometimes the pastor comes down into the aisle for the reading of the Gospel, as a further symbol that the Lord is among his people.

I must confess that I like the high altar, the soaring arches of a Gothic cathedral. My spirit is drawn upward as in prayer, my eyes focused on the altar and cross, perhaps on a painting of our Lord as background. Christ, after all, is "God of God, Light of light," and I am told to "seek the things that are above where Christ is" and to set my mind "on things that are above, not on things that are of earth." On the other hand, I don't forget that Christ emptied himself and became a servant, and that even upon leaving this earth he promised to be in our midst whenever we are gathered in his name. As the Son of Man he is in the thick of our lives. We are his family, and in the bread and wine on the altar he is truly and mysteriously present with us. In church architecture the pendulum seems to swing between the transcendent Lord, on the one hand, and our Brother as near as the air we breathe, on the other.

In many churches the windows tell the story of our faith, either in symbols or in figures from the Bible. Sitting alone in the quiet of an empty church, a person can be reached by many mute sermons. Altar and pulpit hangings, with colors changed for the seasons and festivals of the church year, are reminders of the events and mission in the life of our Lord.

Jeremiah speaks of people "who have eyes, but see not." This could very well be a description of many of us as we worship. There is an eloquence all about us if we but take the time to meditate as we look.

In the year that King Uzziah died I saw the Lord sitting upon a throne, high and lifted up; and his train filled the temple. Above him stood the seraphim; each had six wings; with two he covered his face, and with two he covered his feet, and with two he flew. And one called to another and said, "Holy, holy,

holy is the Lord of hosts; the whole earth is full of
his glory."   Isaiah 6:1-3

My God, how wonderful thou art,
Thy majesty how bright!
How beautiful thy mercy seat
In depths of burning light!

How wonderful, how beautiful
The sight of thee must be—
Thine endless wisdom, boundless pow'r,
And awesome purity!

Yet I may love thee too, O Lord,
Almighty as thou art,
For thou hast stooped to ask of me
The love of my poor heart.
        LBW 524

"When I look at thy heavens, the work of thy fingers,
the moon and the stars which thou hast established,"
then I can well ask why you, of such great power,
should bother with us on this tiny planet. But you
have revealed yourself in Christ, and have given us
the Spirit, so that we are able to trust you as children
trust their father. We thank you for the church that
keeps reminding us constantly of this wonderful
truth. Amen.

15

The One Table

One of the ironies and tragedies of Christendom is that Holy Communion, the simple act of coming to eat and drink at the Lord's invitation, which should have united his family more than any other act, has been the point of its separation. Lutheran altars have been set aside for Lutheran communicants, Catholic altars for Catholics, Episcopal altars for Episcopalians. It has been regarded as a betrayal of the faith to cross over. I posed a possible situation to a venerable pastor friend of mine, "Suppose," I said, "that I was in the army stationed in Greenland for two years. The only chaplain was Baptist. Should I attend his Communion services?" He said, "No. You can be saved without Communion; wait until you get home and commune in your own church."

The practice of separation arises largely from how each church defines the presence of Christ in Holy Communion. The average, faithful worshiper is rarely troubled himself with the question. Since the New Testament offers little light, it is the theologians of the church who have enjoyed sharpening their philosophical tools on the nature of Christ's presence. The best efforts of the scholars, however, cannot remove the mystery. Martin Marty, in his book *The Lord's Supper* says, "Mystery means that if you pull away one veil, another will still cover the subject; and one could pull back veils for all the years that history gives and still not have exposed the subject to clear view. Emphatically, the presence of Christ is such a mystery."

Since we are to love God with all our minds, it is praiseworthy to try to pierce the mystery. But to be neat and inclusive about the Lord's Supper has led to some of the most unloving and cruel practices in the church. Dogmaticians have stood between Christ and his Supper, and in fact have made it their own. At the Evanston Assembly of the World Council of Churches in 1953, Eivand Berggrav, late Lutheran Bishop of Norway, embarrassed his fellow Lutherans by not attending the Lutheran Communion service. When I asked him why he boycotted the service, he said, "The other Communion services invited all who were baptized into Christ and who confessed him as Lord. The Lutheran service was restricted to those who accepted the Lutheran doctrine of the real presence. This was the Supper of our Lord and he did the inviting, not the theologians. That's why I refused to come."

Nor has it always been enough to be Lutheran; you had to be the right kind of Lutheran, belonging to a specific branch of Lutheranism, otherwise you would not be received. This has seemed strange, especially to non-Lutherans, and to many Lutherans themselves, especially since for over 400 years there have been no differences among Lutherans in the interpretation of the Supper itself. There have been other theological differences, in defining the nature of biblical inspiration, for instance, but all Lutheran bodies have confessed a firm consensus on the doctrine of Holy Communion.

Fortunately, many doors have opened in the last two decades, among Lutherans, and beyond, in the whole Christian family. Scholars of most churches have met across denominational barriers to compare their traditions and, often to their delight and surprise, have discovered that once the theological language is carefully examined, they are not very far apart, if at all. I remember one such encounter when a Lutheran theologian returned from a conference to report that the other churches were very close to the Lutheran in their understanding of the Supper. For a moment we were almost frightened; does this mean that our altars should be open to all Christians? Christ might be pleased if they were.

A student from India, much concerned about the unity of Christ's church, sat in my office. I posed a question: Suppose five scholars from five churches—

Roman Catholic, Methodist, Lutheran, Eastern Ortho-
dox, and Episcopal—were gathered to formulate a
common statement about Holy Communion. Where
they met, there were two rooms, one a chapel, the
other a conference room. I asked, "Should they first
go to the conference room and then, after they had
arrived at an agreed statement, come to the chapel
to celebrate Communion; or, should they first go to
the chapel, celebrate the Supper together, each with
his own understanding of Christ's presence, and then
go to work in the conference room?"

He quickly replied, "If they go first to the conference room, they'll never get to the chapel. If they
go first to the chapel and eat and drink the Lord's
body and blood together, they may succeed in the
conference room." Today many are going to the
chapel before the work in the conference room is
finished. As Martin Marty has indicated, the work
in the conference room may never be finished. The
divine mystery of the Supper is too big for words.

This doesn't mean that the work of scholars is un-
important. It would be a pity if no one cared to
probe the profound meanings of Scripture and God's
way with his children. The Christian faith has en-
listed some of the finest minds of the centuries, and
the Spirit has used this work to usher the church into
the riches of the kingdom.

It is my personal hope that the day may come
when, without losing the wealth of the separate traditions and doctrines the Holy Spirit and history
have entrusted to the churches, all Christian altars

will be open to all who worship the Lord in serious-
ness, regardless of denominational memberships. I
like to imagine a long table encircling the earth,
with all of the Lord's followers gathered to receive
the body and the blood together.

*I therefore, a prisoner for the Lord, beg you to lead
a life worthy of the calling to which you have been
called, with all lowliness and meekness, with pa-
tience, forbearing one another in love, eager to main-
tain the unity of the Spirit in the bond of peace.
There is one body and one Spirit, just as you were
called to the one hope that belongs to your call, one
Lord, one faith, one baptism, one God and Father
of us all, who is above all and through all and in
all.*   Ephesians 4:1-6

The Church's one foundation is Jesus Christ, her
   Lord;
She is his new creation by water and the Word.
From heaven he came and sought her to be
   his holy bride,
With his own blood he bought her, and for
   her life he died.

Elect from every nation, yet one o'er all
   the earth;
Her charter of salvation: one Lord, one faith,
   one birth.
One holy name she blesses, partakes one
   holy food,

And to one hope she presses with ev'ry grace
endued.
LBW 369

*As I come to your Table, O Lord, help me to en-
visage a great host, your followers the world over.
Many different from me in many ways, but you died
for them and they have been drawn to you as Lord.
If they are yours, and I am yours, then we are brothers and sisters in the faith. Let me never be guilty of
turning my back on them or elbowing them away
from your Table. Give me the joy of opening my
arms wide to receive them. Amen.*